AMAZING MANDALA COLORING BOOK FOR BEGINNERS

50 Single Sided Beginner Friendly Adult Mandala Coloring Book For Relaxation & Stress Relieve. (Vol. 3)

By
Thrive Coloring

© Copyright 2020

Thrive Coloring Books | All Rights Reserved.

No part of this book or the material in it may be cited from or replicated in any way by means such as printing, scanning, photocopying, or otherwise without the prior written authorization of **Thrive Coloring Books.**

INTERESTED IN THE DIGITAL PDF VERSION

COPY AND PASTE THE LINK BELOW INTO YOUR WEB BROSWER TO BUY THE PRINTABLE DIGITAL PDF VERSION

https://bit.ly/36n8Hfy

HAVE A QUESTION OR CUSTOM REQUEST? LET US KNOW.

EMAIL: info@thrivecoloringbooks.com

WEBSITE: ThriveColoringBooks.com

This Coloring Book Belongs To:

_____

_____

_____

DID YOU ENJOYED COLORING THIS MANDALA BOOK

IF YES, THEN SHARE THE LOVE WITH YOUR FRIENDS AND FAMILIES OR GIFT THEM ONE AND LET THEM ALSO CONTINUE THE FUN

IF YOU ENJOYED COLORING THIS BOOK, TAKE A PICTURE OF YOUR LOVELY COLORING PAGE AND SHARE IT TO THE WORLD ON AMAZON

KINDLY TYPE THE LINK BELOW INTO YOUR WEB BROWSER TO WRITE A FEEDBACK ON AMAZON

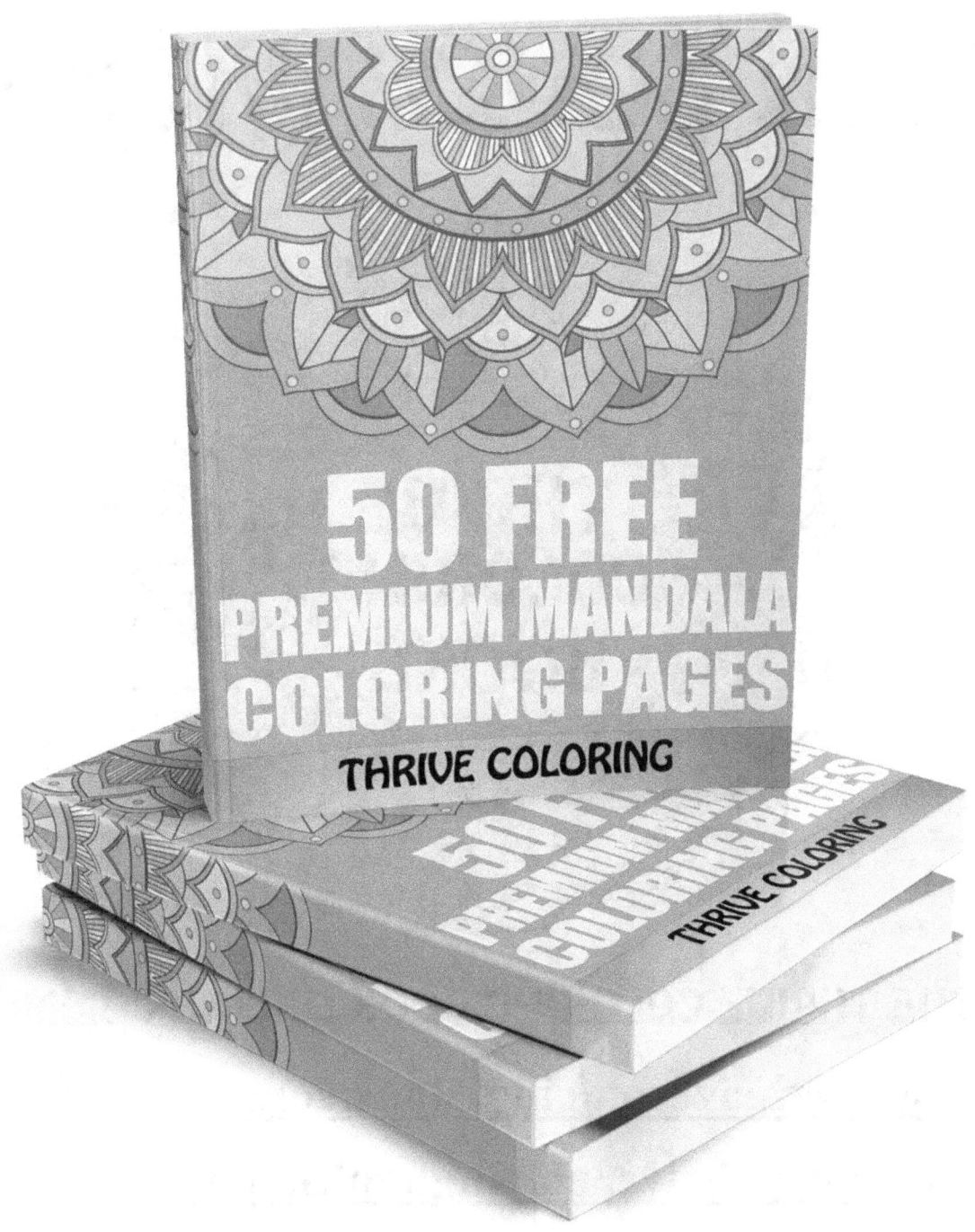

DOWNLOAD YOUR FREE COPY OF 50 PREMIUM MANDALA COLORING PAGES

http://bit.ly/2Qupg2n

GET IN TOUCH WITH US

JOIN THE THRIVE COLORING BOOK ONLINE COMMUNITY

EMAIL: **info@thrivecoloringbooks.com**

WEBSITE: **www.thrivecoloringbooks.com**

FACEBOK: **@thrivecoloringbooks**

PINTEREST: **@thrivecoloringbooks**

AMAZON: **Amazon.com/Author/ThriveColoringBooks**